Matthew T. Stolte

John M. Bennett

DRILLING FOR SUIT MYSTERY

© Matthew Stolte & John M. Bennett 2012

(also with C. Mehrl Bennett in Section Two collaborations)

Book design by C. Mehrl Bennett

ISBN: 1-892280-92-2

13 Digit ISBN: 978-1-892280-92-3

LUNA BISONTE PRODS

137 Leland Ave.

Columbus, OH 43214 USA

www.johnmbennett.net

http://www.lulu.com/spotlight/lunabisonteprods

LUNA BISONTE PRODS

2012

SECTION ONE: Matthew T. Stolte
John M. Bennett (2011)

ME .. 8.11

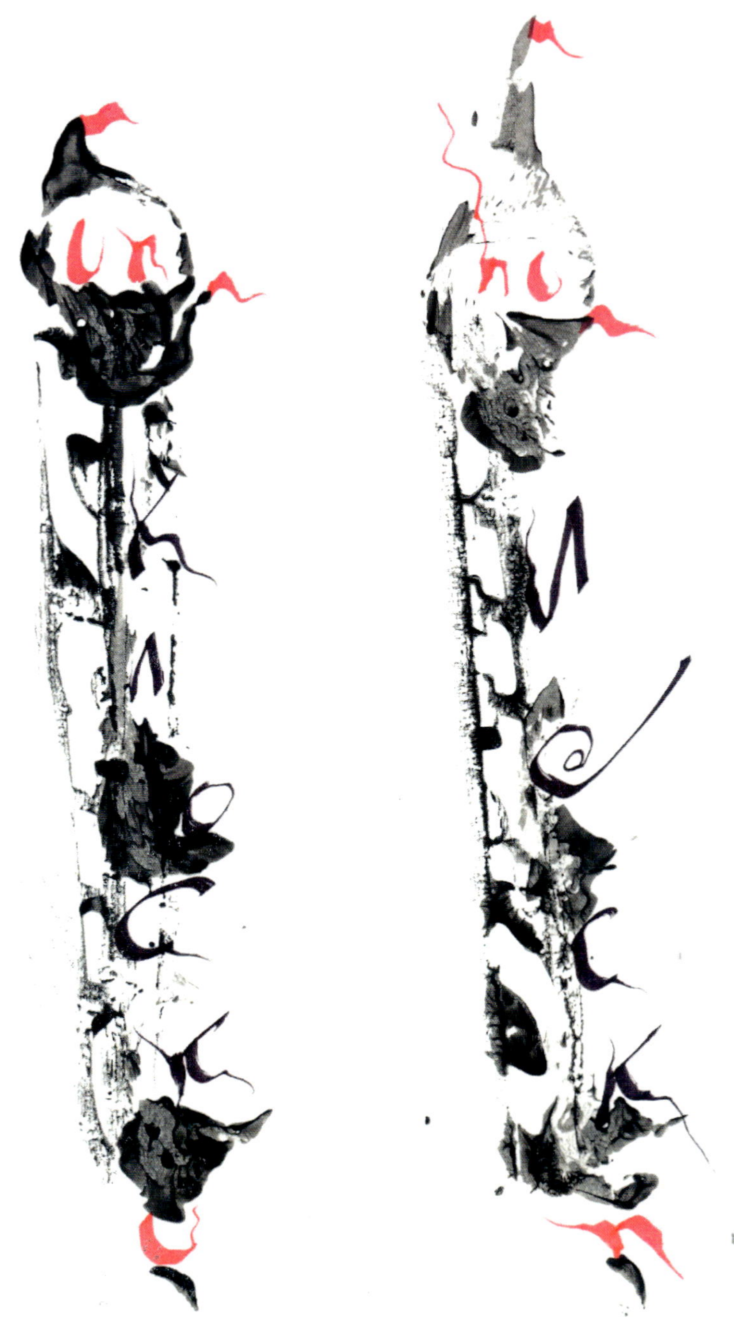

MB ..8.11

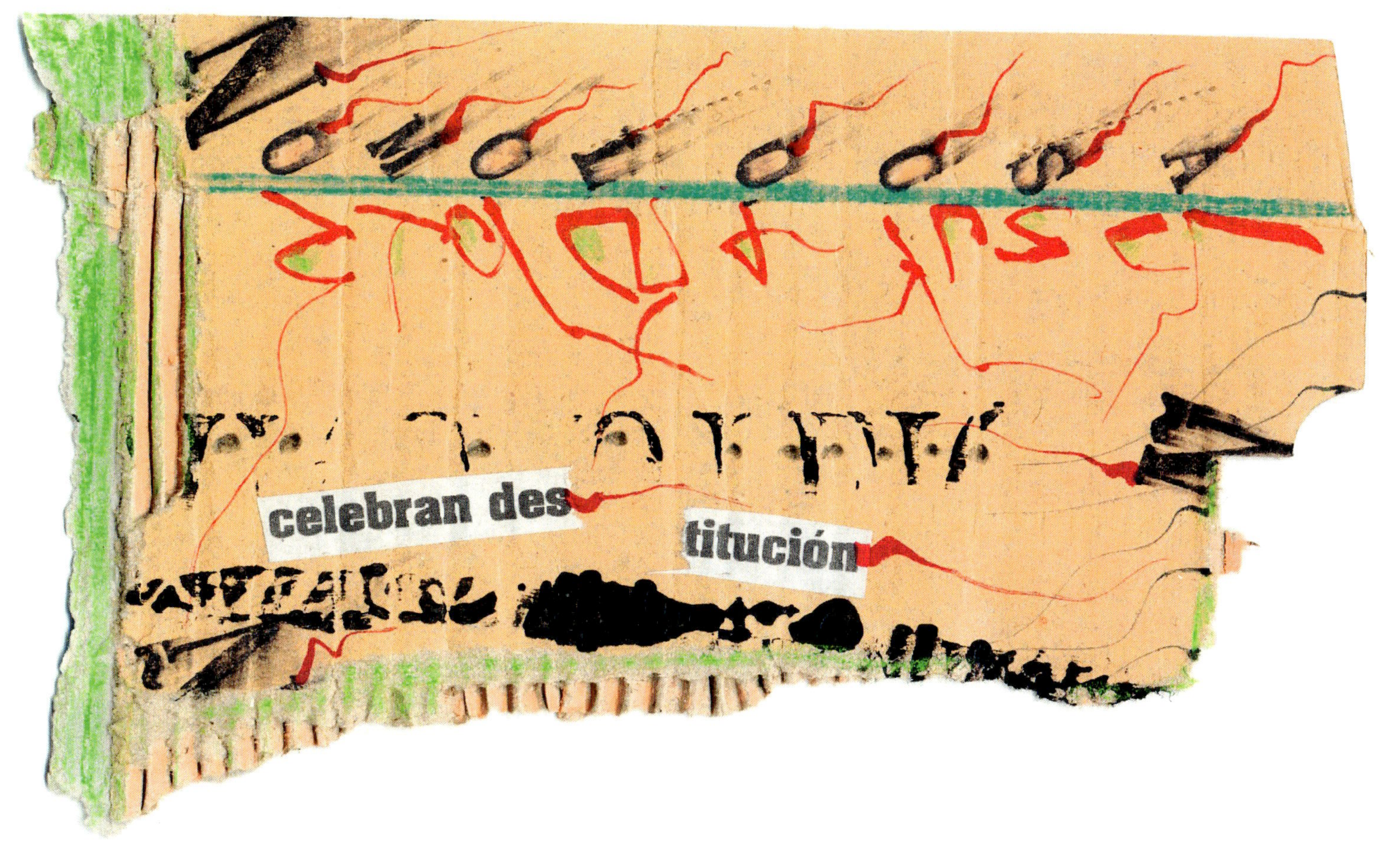

celebran des
titución

I wanted
duffle bag.
chiefly on the floor,
included a rack
had happened
dirty dishes,
three small boxes
and for a
no pygmies in South America.
pink garbage
a number
oud split.
reverie.
books,
impedimenta.

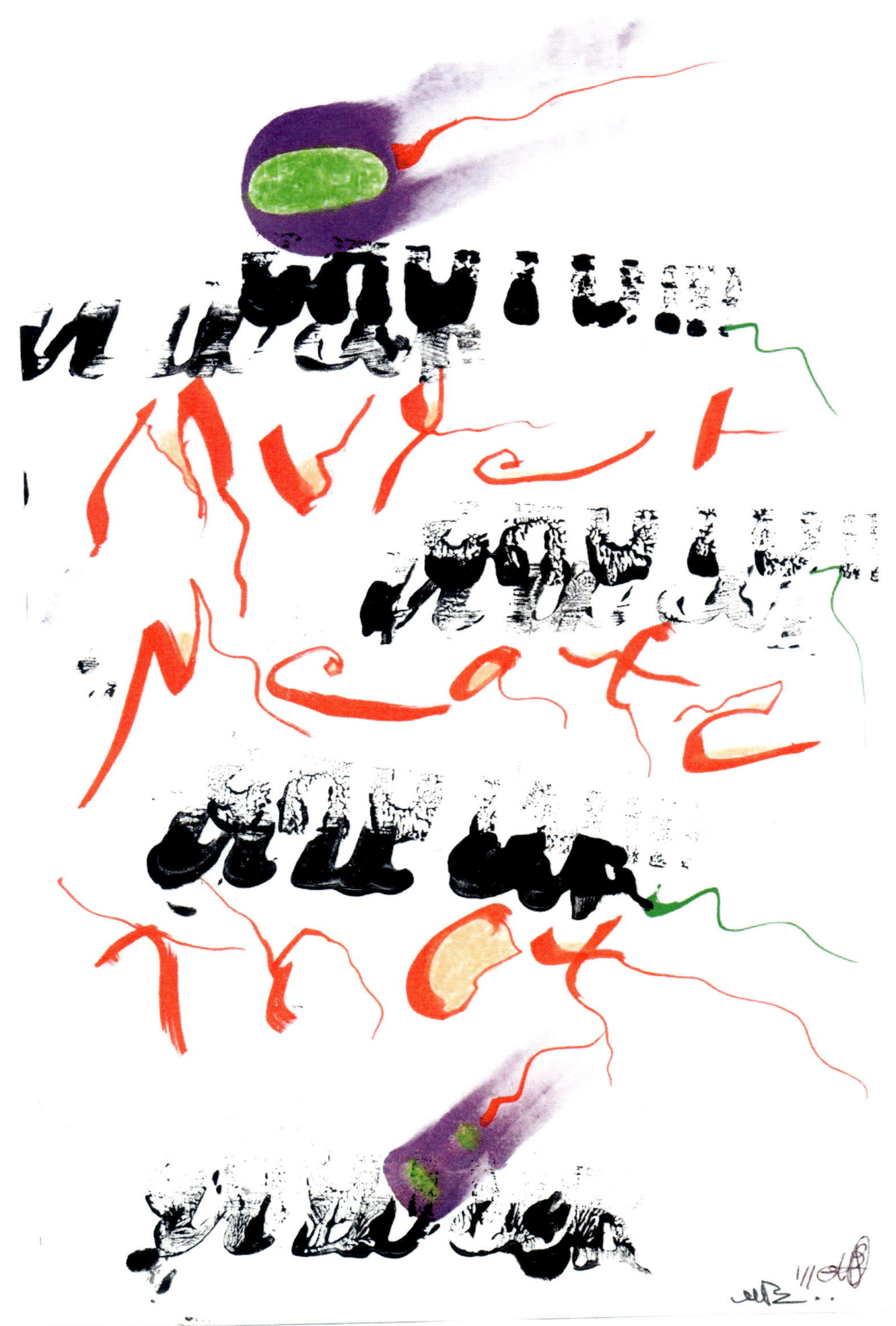

CIUDAD AZTECA
TOWING
we

Stop the Nazis!

ST
re
WE'LL
IF
THE

Syfy
H
mano armada

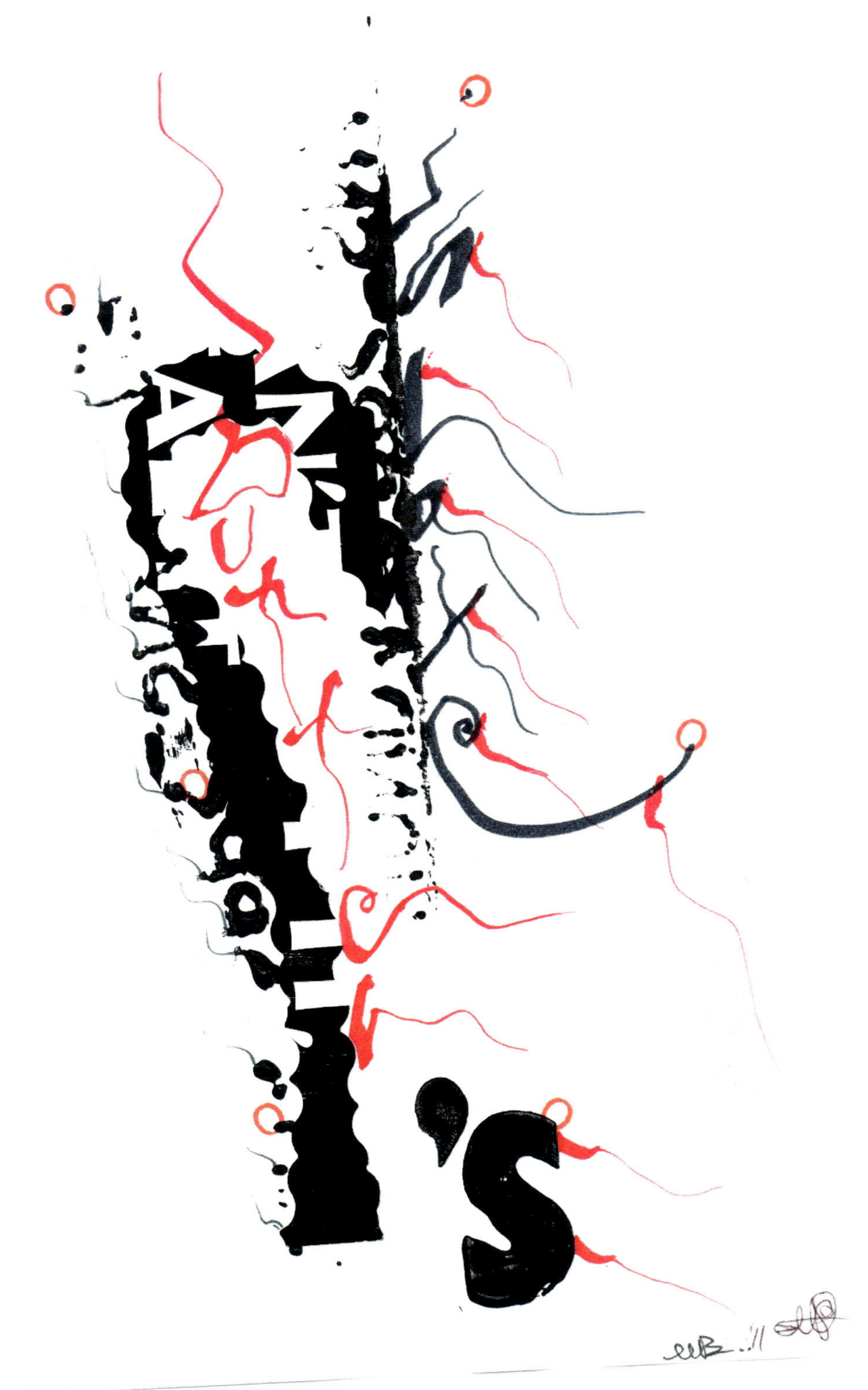

norma

en accidente
ut the People Movement at 313-559-7074
Take the 18 or 76 bus.

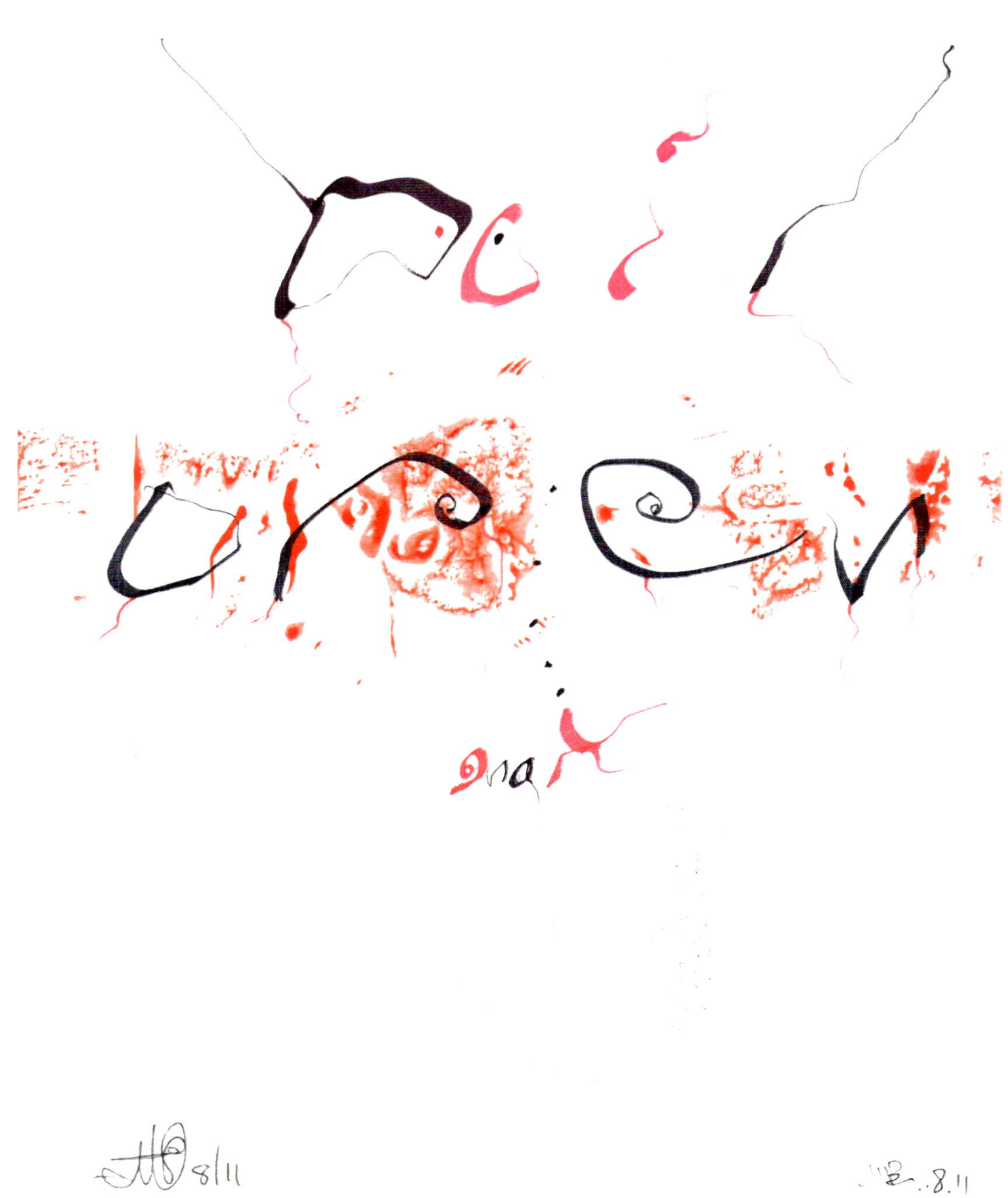

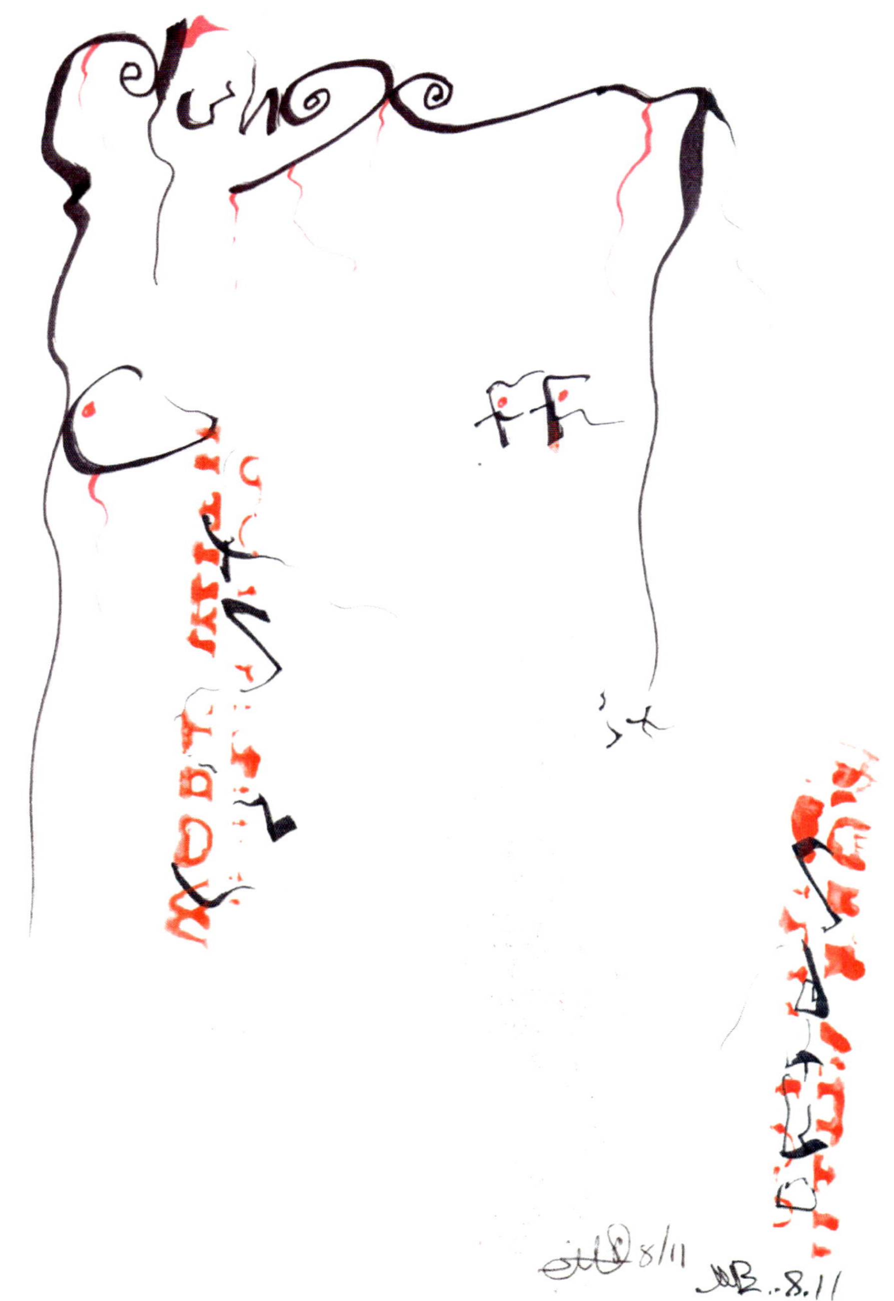

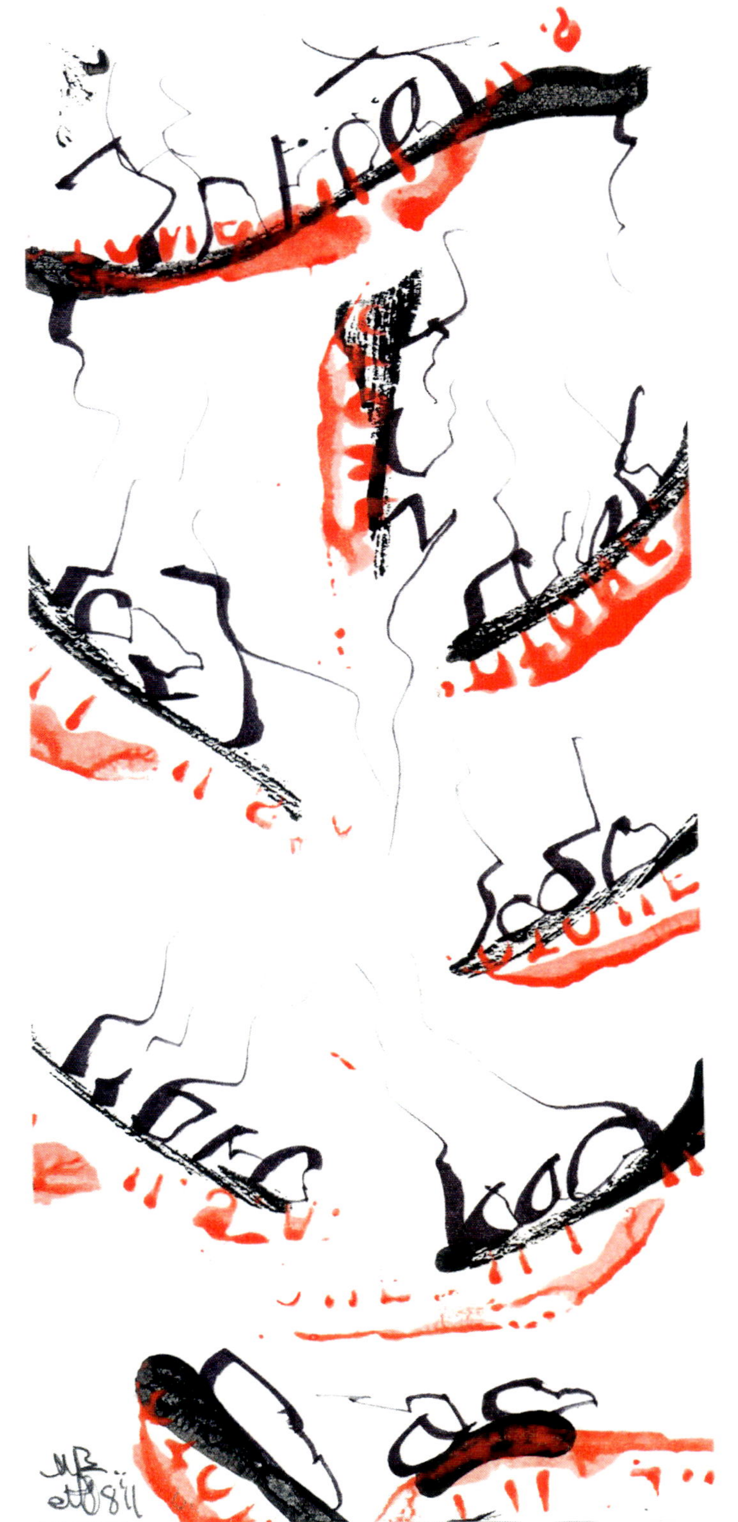

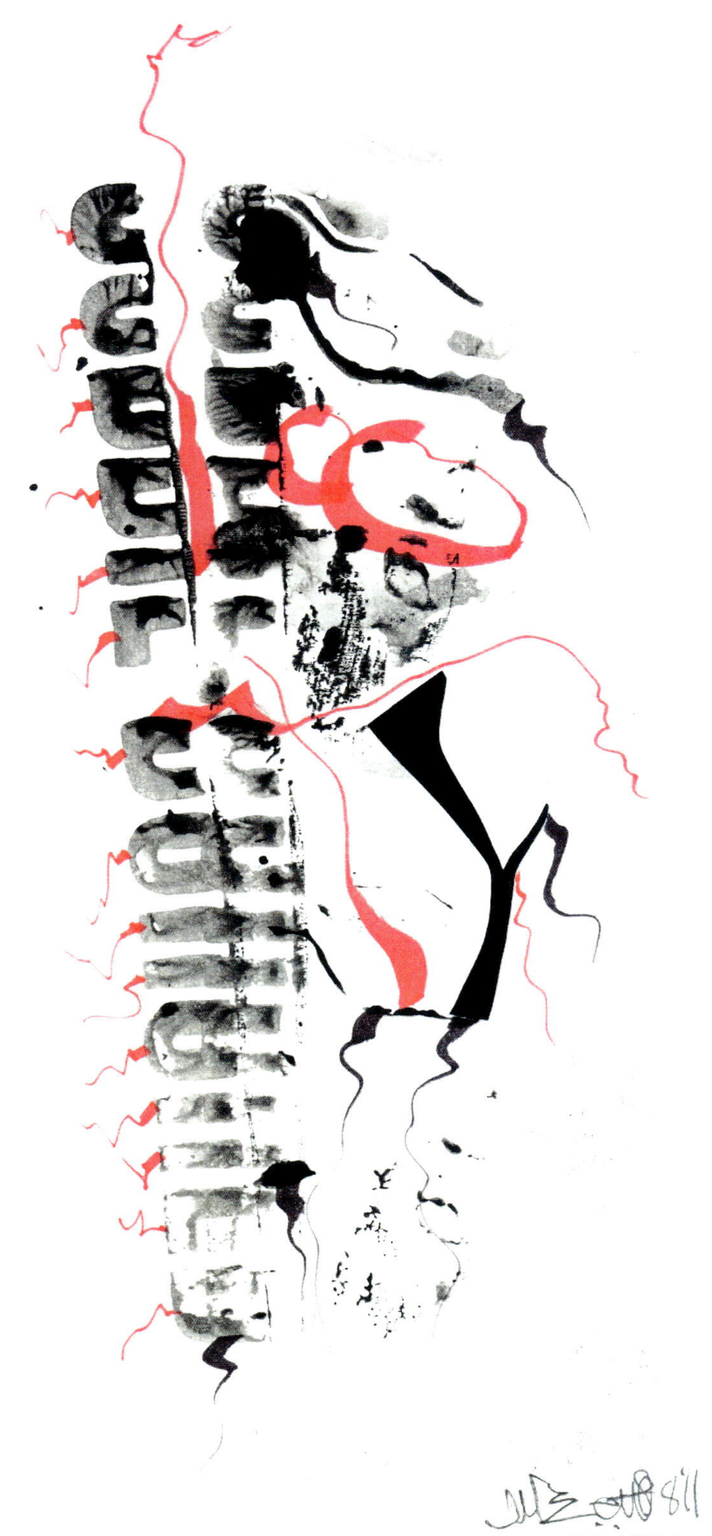

blanca
visible
jowl with a bag

easily with a stick to hel,
door with the dogs crow
RR
R
R
R
R
R
saco goteante

g
N
*nadir (nā' dẽr), n. the part of
directly under the place where
opposed to zenith.

stood dead still in fro
OT REMOVE SA
UNIT HAS BE
maintains the cor

TU
titulada "tu humo" dedal
o logomado te llevas el

as a cow
se suddenly,
s the idea of having existed or
only a short time; novel impi
t to turn;
s turning
is good

nd wheeling over
m the remains of
or the fact that if her will
lly back from the depths

sh feet waver sh
sh snort sh
sh

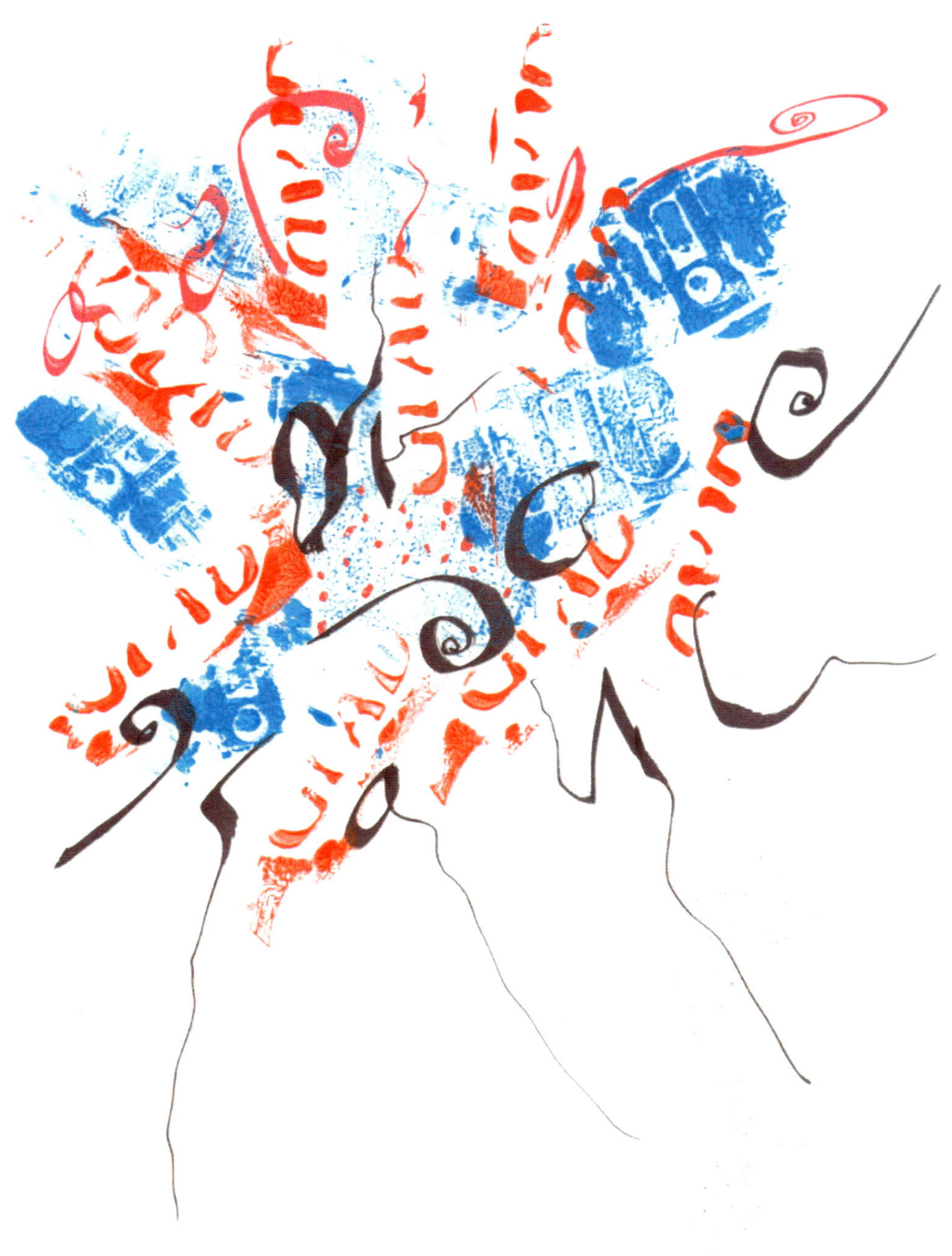

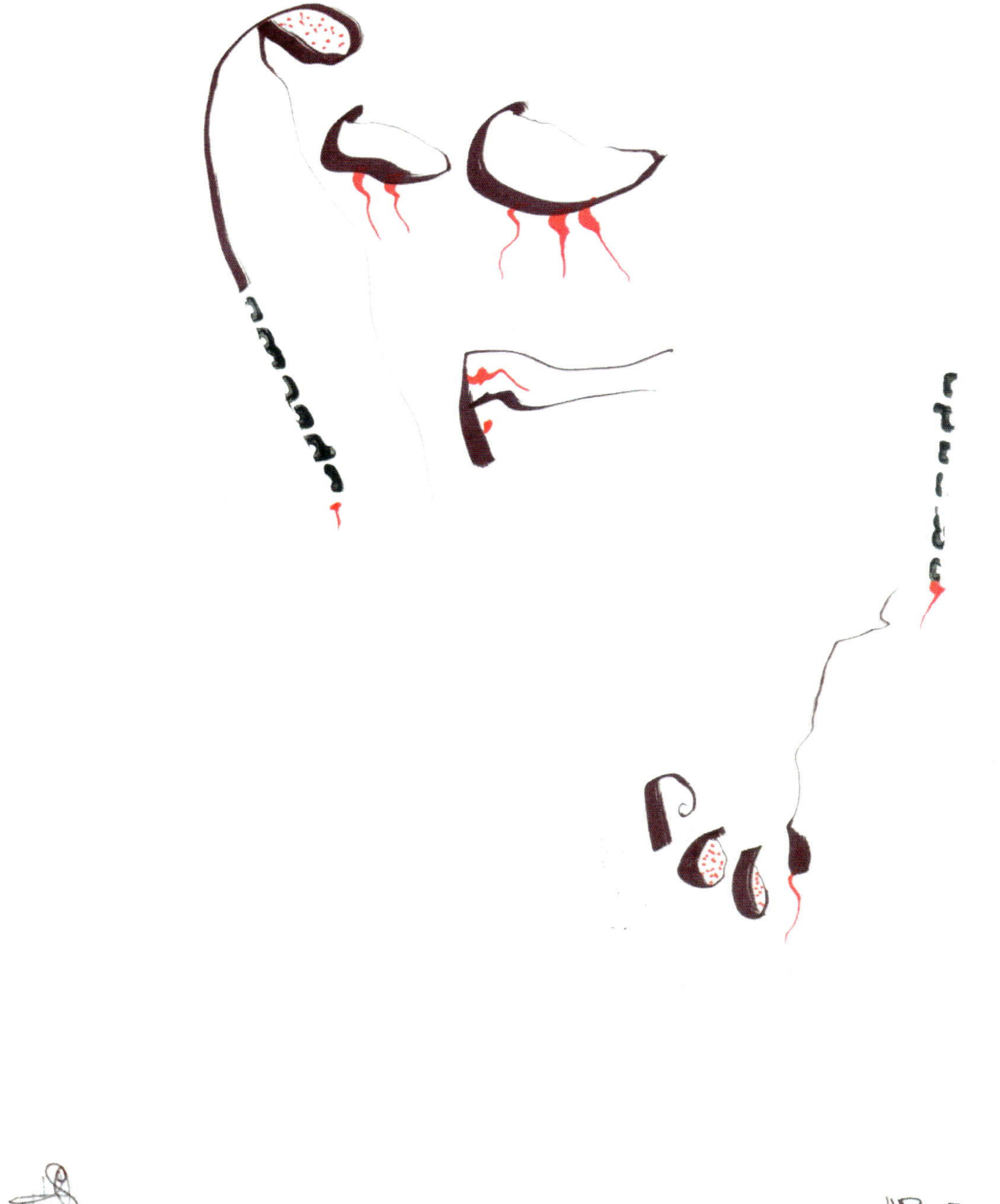

SECTION TWO: Matthew T. Stolte
John M. Bennett
C. Mehrl Bennett (2011)

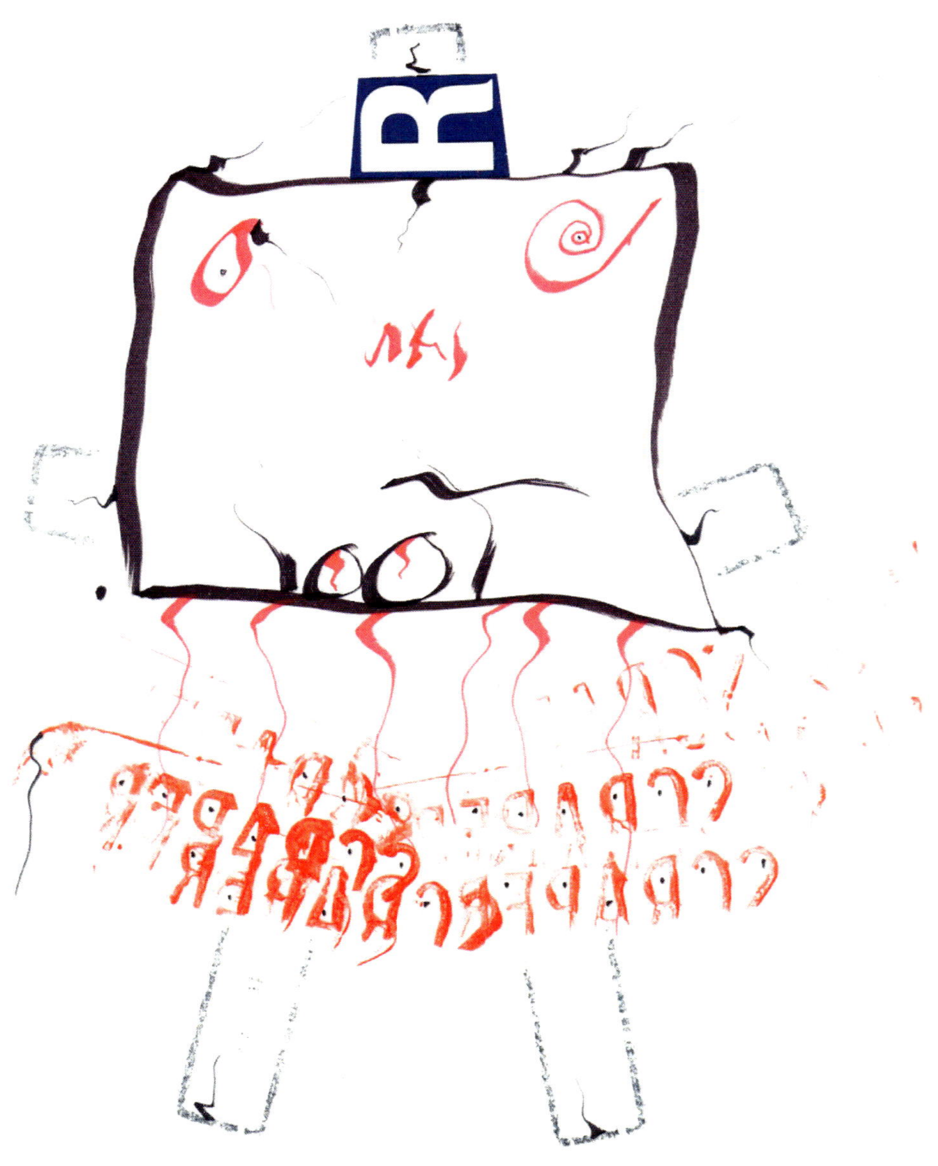

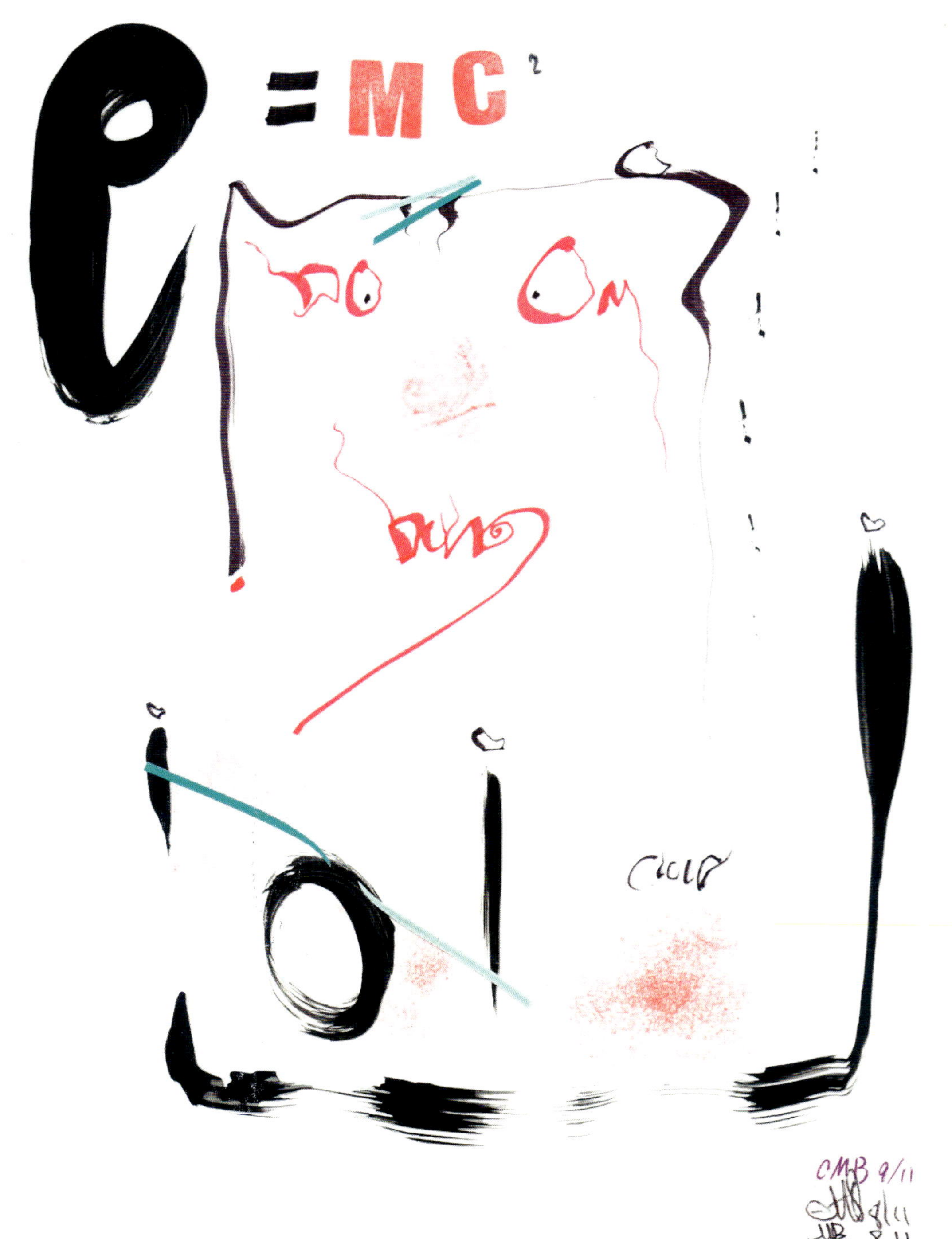

$E = MC^2$

AUCTION
AUCTION - 11:00
Original art by Peter Max, Doll, Rockwell, Turkey and many more.
JEWELRY, ROLEX and other flashy items DULY instructed by Millionaire as well as other prominent traders. Seized assets and general order merchandise will be auctioned off to the highest bidder to recover losses from PONZI SCHEME.
www.madoffhelpline.com
Items available for auction did not belong to Bernie Madoff but are being offered by victims of the ponzi scheme to recoup losses. 15% Buyers Premium
DUE TO LOSSES CAUSED BY
BERNIE MADOFF
SUNDAY DECEMBER 20
AM, PREVIEW 10:30
EMBASSY SUITES HOTEL
DUBLIN, OH

CMB 9.11

KIMONO
MYSTERY
MYSTERY

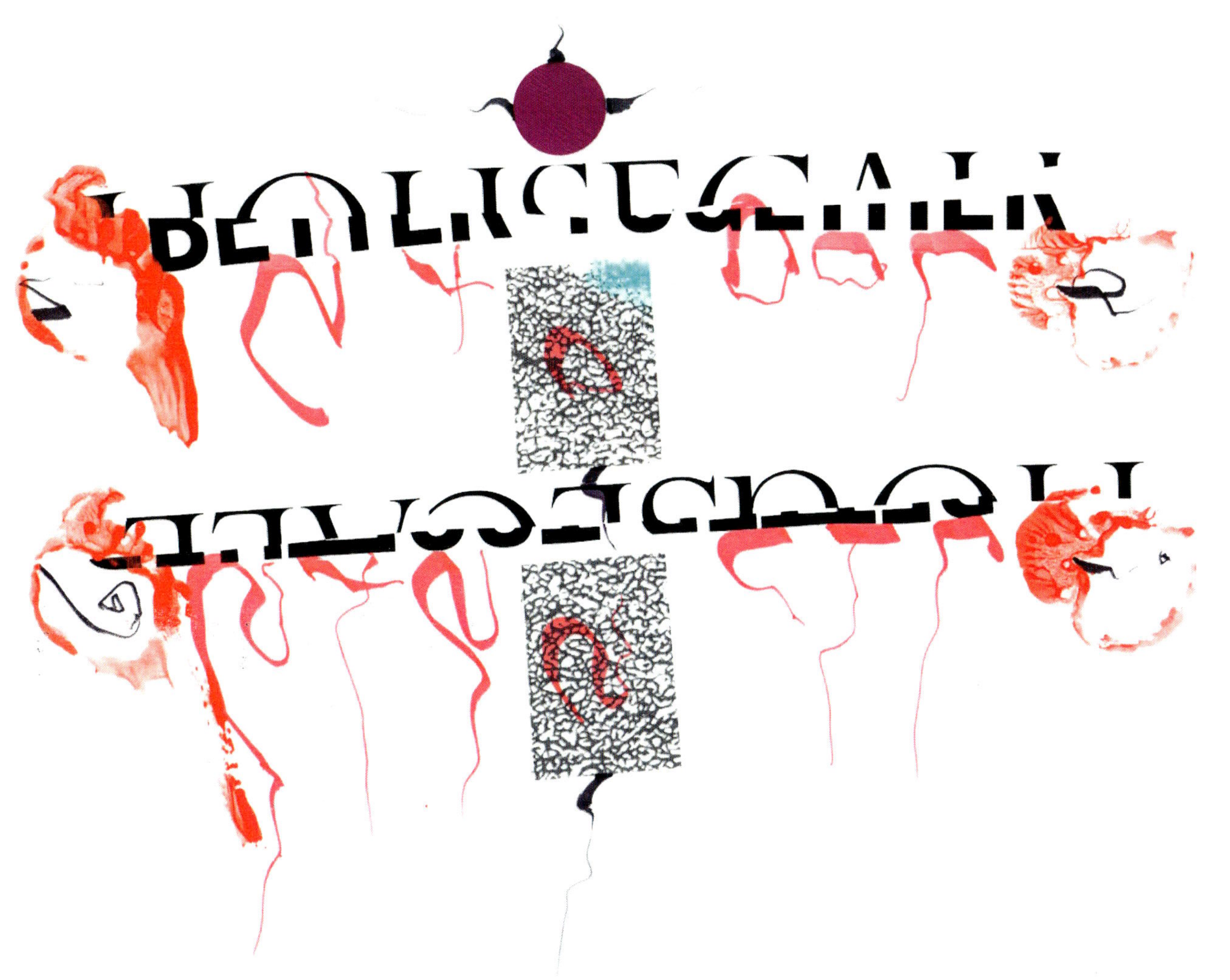

DRILLING FOR
oil

EW
U
CMB 9.11

SECTION THREE: Matthew T. Stolte
John M. Bennett (2012)

de pruebas.
er nuevos in-
a su lugar de
BEE
of numbers fogged in my pocket 1
LO

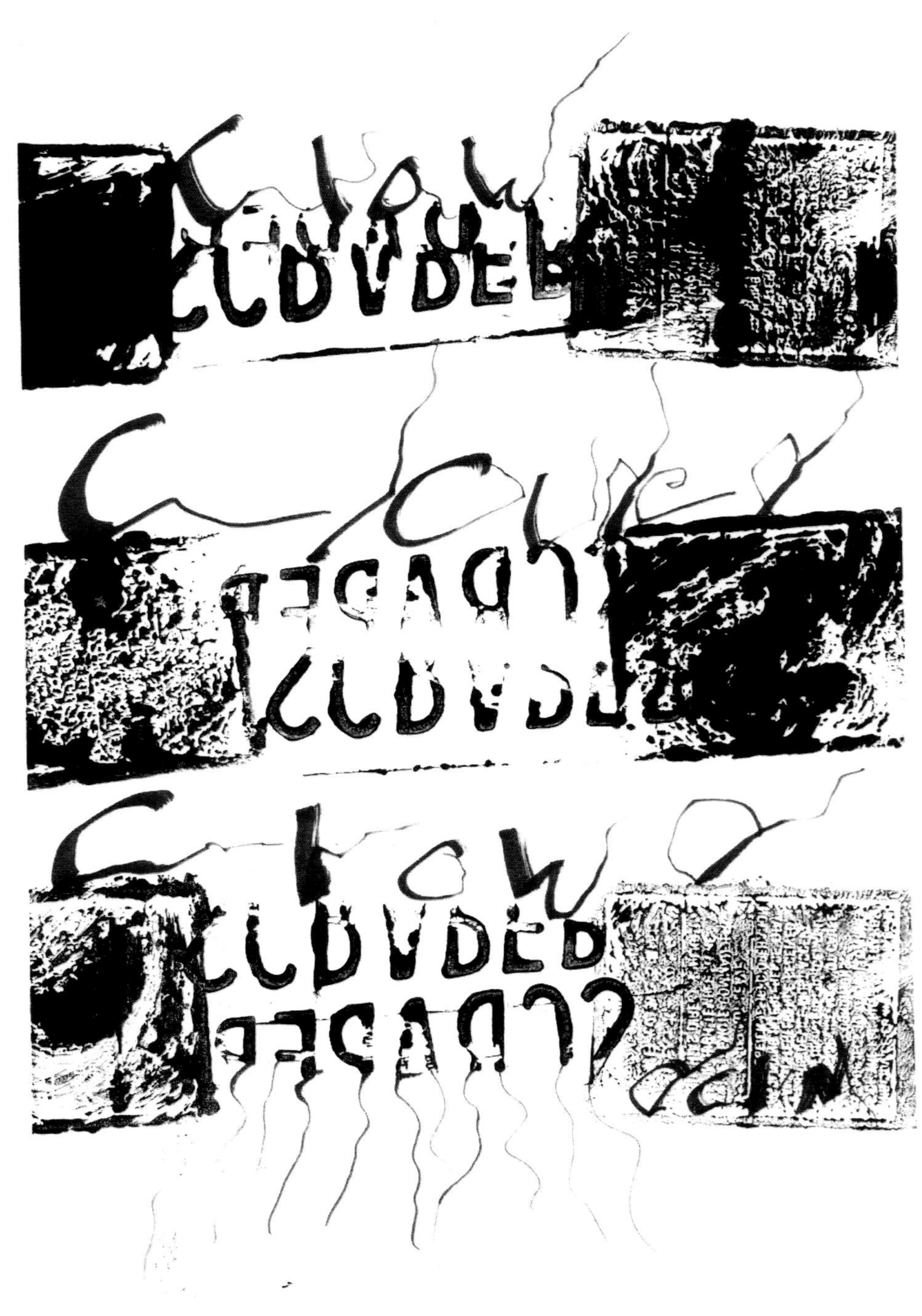

coat dogged the
where I was the wind

wind your glasses retained my

cradled a wind in a darkened street

real trouble. He was

South. vermouth.

screeching to a
halt. ass
umlaut.

the crusted wind I covered with

cactus. past

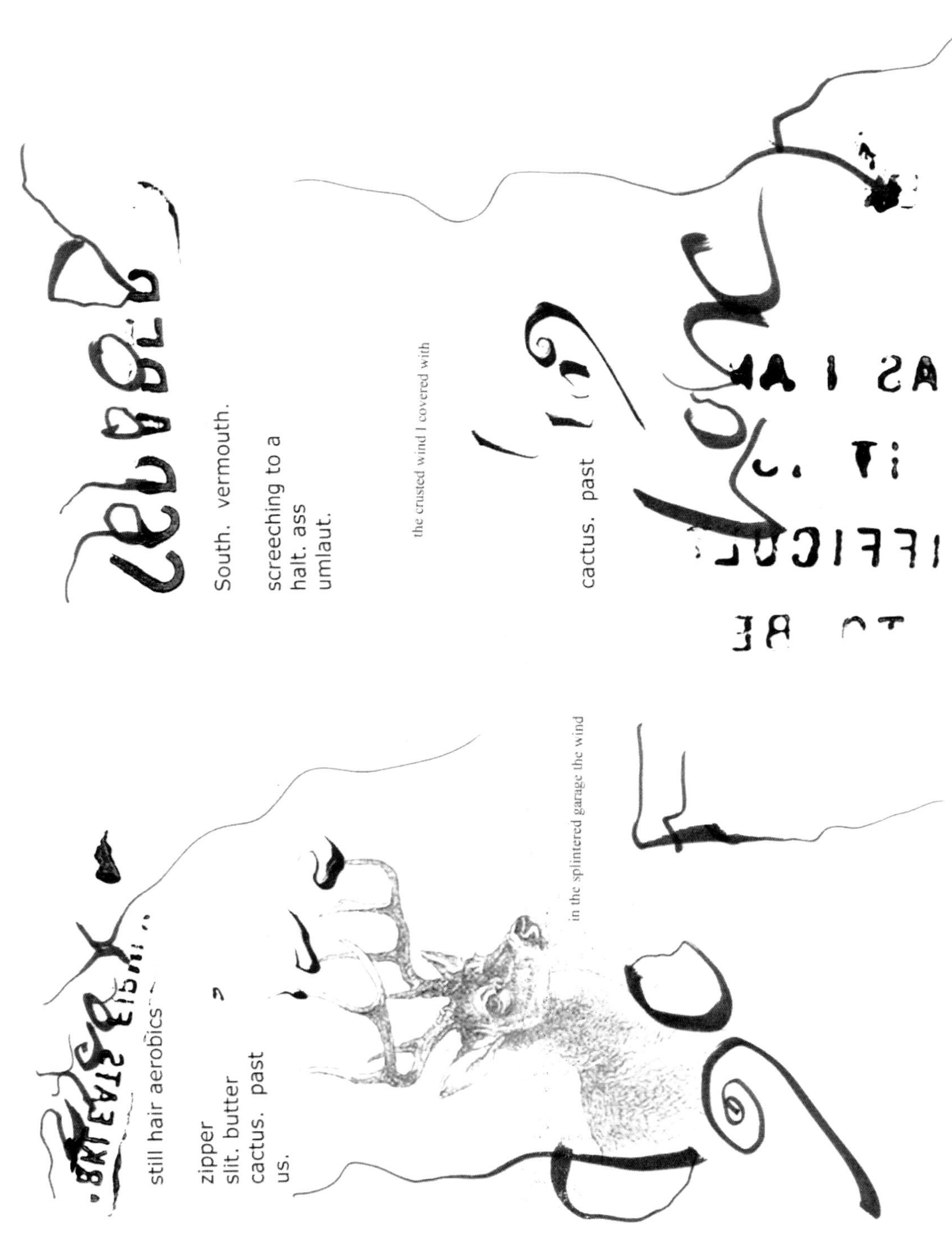

still hair aerobics

zipper
slit. butter
cactus. past
us.

"little shit"
Kill neck sister pater stress aimant merde y whore
Les sister chevaux de trait le net par je trou dément mélicoliux
Il m'excite le net pas tu dément mélicoliux
Ile nègre size tpi de Cree tu m'aimais Tallahasse
Lucien Suel
from people and
fibers from clothing and carp
Coe said. That dust usually is pre
microns o
trains mount me to the slow drink
hard in the mud
the act of using tobacco in a pipe, cigar or
cigarette, as this is a good smoke.
(smok), v.t. and v.t. to give out
Nickel And
stockings
sugaring
little
taNks Smell
Hat
It
ALED for YOUR SEALED for YOUR
ROTECTION PROTECTION
what you say
the matter
paper to
correct
with
take

sandwich hollowed with wind and

bla
truck